Elements of Design

SPACE

Although this space appears to be outdoors, it is really a fantastic interior space — the atrium-lobby of a hotel. The sculpture in the center of the space is four stories high. Photo courtesy of the Hyatt Regency Hotel in San Francisco.

Elements of Design

SPACE

Gerald F. Brommer

Art Teacher, Lutheran High School
Los Angeles, California

DAVIS PUBLICATIONS, INC.
Worcester, Massachusetts

Other Books by Gerald F. Brommer:

Wire Sculpture and Other Three-Dimensional
  Construction
Relief Printmaking
Drawing: ideas, materials and techniques
Transparent Watercolor: ideas and techniques

Printed in the United States of America
Library of Congress Catalog Card Number: **74-82680**
ISBN 0-87192-062-x

Printing: Davis Press
Type: 10 point Theme Medium
Graphic Design: Thumbnail Associates

Consulting Editors: George F. Horn, Sarita R. Rainey

10 9 8 7 6 5 4 3

CONTENTS

INTRODUCTION

People seeking an awareness to design often turn to nature as a source for ideas. This is a prime source but not the only one available to us. We are surrounded by man-made materials, buildings and products that can stimulate sound thinking in design.

You do not exist in nature alone. Nor do you function solely in a world of man-made materials or products. Both are part of your environment and are excellent sources for design ideas.

When talking about paintings or products, you should be able to communicate about design and the relative merits of designed objects.

Communication requires a language — and the language of visual art is *design*. Before you can discuss design, you must be familiar with the elements of art: line, shape, form, space, color, value and texture. Before you can form valid conclusions about the design merit of objects around you, you need to be conversant in the principles of design: balance, emphasis, rhythm, movement, unity, proportion, contrast and pattern.

Design is everywhere! From the marching lines of telephone poles to the orderly displays of vegetables and fruit in the supermarket. From the surface pattern of a skyscraper to the colors on the billboards at the corner. Designers are trying to catch your eye, hold your interest and make their product attractive. Organizing materials to produce the most effective product is *designing*.

The elements of design are the raw materials of the designer . . . the visual components of art. Look for them in the lines of a tile floor, the shapes of windows and doors, the form of a bus or candy bar, the color of your house, the values in the tree outside your room or the texture of your sweater.

The principles of design will help you coordinate these elements to produce effective visual results.

This book attempts to help you become more aware of one of the design elements — space.

I have just returned from a trip through space. Actually, so have you. When you walked to the shelf to pick up this book, you were walking in space. Space is all around you. . . Sometimes crowded — sometimes open. It may be full of trees or buildings, clouds or clear air. It can be contained by walls or open to the horizons. We move in space — running, walking or driving. Forward, back, around, under, behind, over, into, out from, can all indicate action taken in space.

Trying to show space in a painting or drawing presents some problems. This book will help you become aware of ways to indicate depth or space in your work. Many spatial concepts are shown and others are discussed but they are just a beginning. Start from these concepts and build your own vocabulary of spatial ideas by looking carefully around you. Your environment holds the answers to many of your questions about visual space.

TWO-DIMENSIONAL SPACE

Look at the floor. . . it is flat. A table top, sheet of cardboard, plywood or canvas board are also flat. They can be described in terms of two dimensions — height and width.

Since a flat sheet of paper has no depth, we call it a two-dimensional surface. We could fold the paper to make it three-dimensional, or we might draw on it to produce an illusion of some three-dimensional form. But the *flat* sheet of paper is simply a two-dimensional surface, perhaps twelve inches high by eighteen inches wide.

Positive and negative space

If you put a black square on the flat white paper, you get a new feeling. The surface is still two-dimensional, but it is now divided into black and white spaces; the black shape seen against a white background. The square is a positive shape and the white area around it is a negative space.

Add a few more black shapes and the feeling changes. You see several black positive spaces and an encompassing white negative space.

Generally the bolder color spaces will appear positive against a more neutral background. At times it is difficult to tell which space is positive and which is negative with some artists taking pleasure in deceiving the eye by creating an optical illusion.

The picture plane

The surface on which an artist works whether it be paper, board, canvas or Masonite is called the picture plane. Since *plane* means flat, we assume the artist will begin on a flat two-dimensional surface.

It is difficult to create much actual depth on a canvas. Vincent Van Gogh did it with thick applications of paint (impasto) and a collage artist might build up a relief surface with cardboard or paper. But generally our drawings and paintings appear flat.

Some artists and designers do not try to achieve an illusion of three dimensions; they would rather make their art appear perfectly flat. Other painters want their work to have a feeling of depth and they manipulate all the elements of art to produce a sense of depth — a three-dimensional effect. You might produce illusions of depth (see pages 12 to 15) but the picture plane remains flat.

When flat shapes touch each other on the picture plane, the space is compressed and a flatness occurs.

Overlapping the shapes would produce a feeling of depth.

Outlined shapes also tend to appear flat when no shadows are thrown or no shading appears on the shapes. Calligraphy and lettering also seem to produce a flat two-dimensional feeling.

If an artist wants to emphasize the two-dimensional quality of the picture plane, he can use one or all of these devices to make his point.

10

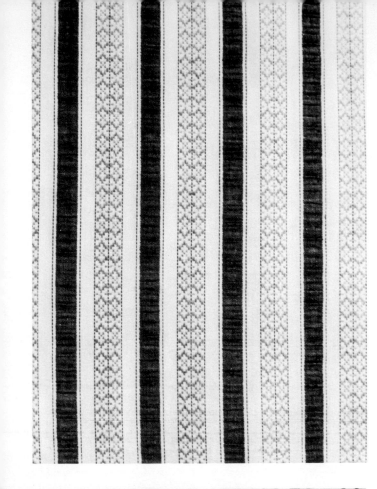

Close values and patterns equal flatness

When values (darks and lights) are closely related, there appears to be a flattening of space. None of the shapes seems to exert itself to move forward or backward and the design remains two-dimensional.

Closely related colors (near each other on the color wheel) will do the same thing. Orange, yellow-orange and red-orange shapes, if nearly the same in value, will tend to lie flat on the picture plane. Contrasting colors will show evidence of depth, because the warmer and brighter colors will seem to come forward.

A picture plane covered with pattern presents an impression of eliminating a feeling of depth and feels flat. By repeating shapes, lines or colors in a regular system, a strong feeling of two-dimensional space is developed. If designers want to emphasize the concept of flatness, they can use close-valued patterns and related colors to eliminate the slightest sense of three-dimensional space.

The illusion of depth in art

By using many of the techniques described in the following pages, you can create a sense of three dimensions on a flat picture plane. Artists have been doing this for centuries and their methods have been startlingly similar over this stretch of time.

If the flat shapes in the examples on previous pages are overlapped, a third dimension is evident — depth. Making some shapes smaller than others will produce a similar effect as will making some values darker than others. Converging lines will also cause your mind to read a third dimension into the design.

When your two-dimensional work requires a three-dimensional feeling, look at the way a camera sees the three-dimensional world around you and let it help you solve your problems. The following pages filled with camera observations of that world (your environment) should get you started.

A an AARDVARK IS A SOUTH AFRICAN GROUND-HOG

Charcoal sketch of a still life uses overlapping forms and shadows to create a sense of space.

The artist has created a feeling of space on a flat sheet of paper by having lines converge at a point in the distance. The charcoal sketch of Puerto Vallarta is by Ralph Hulett, who has also used value contrasts to help create the illusion of depth.

14

Shadows on the rocks give a feeling of form and the over-lapping rocks create a sense of depth. Rocks in the forefront show details, while trees and cliff in the distance are lacking detail, adding to the feeling of three-dimensional space. The watercolor painting is absolutely flat but the feeling is one of space.

*Solid sculptures of varied size or material exist in space. Space surrounds them, sometimes not quite penetrating their mass. Consider this negative space as an important part of sculpture. Try thinking of the **shape of the space** as much as the form of the sculpture or building.*

THREE-DIMENSIONAL SPACE

Most downtown skyscrapers are solid masses and usually are enclosed rectilinear forms. Often they are surrounded by other skyscrapers so that their encompassing space cannot be noticed. This building is relatively alone and you can **feel** the space around it.

Eight hundred-foot high Spider Rock in Canyon de Chelly is a towering monolithic form. The space enveloping Spider Rock is easily noticeable because it is contained in a canyon that has 1000-foot high walls. The deep shadows emphasize the feeling of solidity and space.

When we use words like into, over, under, around, behind or surrounding, we are speaking of three-dimensional space. Literally, another dimension has been added to the two-dimensional plane — that of actual depth. In this three-dimensional realm we are looking for solidity, volume and mass. We can physically walk around a three-dimensional sculpture or downtown building.

Yet we are not concerned *only* with the object we create or one at which we look but we want to notice its surrounding space. We are as much concerned with the negative as the positive, as much with the space around as with the object itself. When we walk around that three-dimensional sculpture, we are walking in the space that surrounds it. That space is a vital part of the object itself.

Space around things

Solid forms such as buildings, flagpoles or monolithic mountains are three-dimensional — they occupy space. We can move around them. We are not often conscious of the space surrounding such solid objects, especially if that space seems unlimited. When it is contained, as in a stadium or skyscraper-lined street, we become more aware of it. We become acutely aware of it when it is filled with smog, dust or fog, creating an effect of solid space.

17

Space flows through and around the form of the trombone but cannot penetrate the human form itself. Yet the positioning of the fingers can produce forms that can be punctured by space.

18

Space both surrounds and flows through the pierced forms of this wire sculpted bird. The relationship of space and form has produced a balanced sculpture that is pleasing in its design.

The telephone pole, cross arms and wires provide an extremely open form, almost a series of three-dimensional lines. When forms are so open, it is difficult to feel the shape of the spaces involved.

Space flowing through things

Three-dimensional forms that are pierced with holes or are wiry in construction will be penetrated by space. Air will actually become an integral part of the structures or forms, occupying interior spaces in them.

Holes connect one side of the form with the other. Our eyes move into, around and out of the open spaces so that the shapes of these spaces become important to the form itself. A balanced relationship develops — space invades the form and the form occupies its surrounding space.

Irregular organic spaces occupy the areas between the branches of this partially dead tree. Air flows through and around the total form and seems not to be contained by it because of the protrusions the tree makes in its surrounding space.

19

Open space

Traveling in the southwestern part of the United States we often speak of the "wide open spaces." And, they are just that. Sometimes nothing punctuates the horizon for miles and we become acutely aware of sky and space. Clouds might fill the space, but when the clouds disappear, the feeling of vast openness returns.

Looking out over an ocean or a lake can give the same feeling of open space. Airplanes or boats can temporarily interrupt the space but openness will again take over.

The ultimate in open space is our view of the universe — or the view of Earth from outer space. Both views involve huge expanses of open space with little or no obstruction.

A small speedboat makes a momentary intrusion into this open space, while clouds occupy part of the air space above the lake. The darker clouds are closer to us, as are the darker mountains. The water seems to flatten out as it gets farther away from us. Both illusions help produce a feeling of depth or space.

Desert views expose vast distances of unoccupied space. The few telephone poles and even the distant mountains hardly interrupt the feeling of openness. Notice the value change in the sky from light at the horizon to dark above. This is part of the perspective of the sky and produces a three-dimensional feeling of space. A single value from top to bottom would produce a flatness in the sky.

Congested space

In our world today, we are probably more aware of space that is filled with something than of space that seems empty. Our city spaces are crowded with buildings and people. Our roadways or driving spaces are choked with automobiles. Our living spaces are filled with furniture and our wall spaces are decorated with posters and memorabilia. The space under the hood of our car contains a variety of shapes and forms — things to make it run.

When you walk into a forest you are not really conscious of the space the whole forest occupies but only of the space *between* the trees or shrubs. Walking into an elevator with other people makes you aware of the lack of openness — the fullness of the enclosed area. It is congested space.

Getting very close to some things might give you the feeling of congestion because they are made up of many parts crowded together. Yet a tree or tractor found in a large open space can almost appear lonely.

The space that this tractor occupies is congested with mechanical parts that must be placed correctly for greatest efficiency. Designers work carefully to put everything into its correct space both for appearance and efficiency.

Stadiums hold thousands of people that occupy the seating space. Architects have provided an orderly arrangement of rows, aisles and access routes so that the congestion is not oppressive.

Grass might not seem to occupy much space, but if you look at a clump closely, the space **inside** can be quite congested.

The space in a forest seems almost completely filled with trunks, branches and leaves. Yet there is air space or the trees would die. The space is congested, yet breathes because of the open spaces that are still present.

23

*Looking past the girders in the foreground and past the street light, we **know** that the distant buildings are a block or more away. We visually can **feel** the depth of the space.*

Deep space

The depth or shallowness of space is a relative thing. A foot is deeper than an inch but a mile is deeper than the foot. Depth is visually felt when objects of a known size, such as mountains, skyscrapers or people seem tiny in the distance. We *know* they are far away and the smaller they appear the deeper the space.

When astronauts shoot pictures of the earth and it looks like a Ping-Pong ball, the depth is tremendous. This is because we *know* the size of the earth is huge. (See photo on page 20.)

Often objects of a known size seen in the foreground help to create the illusion of deep space because they give a sense of scale to the total scene. Looking *past* foreground objects provides a strong feeling of depth because we *know* that space is between us and the more distant objects.

Lines converging to a point produce a feeling of depth. When
the plants almost disappear in the distance, the sense of **deep**
space is felt immediately.

Leaves and branches are recognized sizes, so the depth of space
between them and the distant figures can be **felt.** You are
looking **past** some forms to see others, which produces a sense
of space.

Pavement and sign are both known factors, so the mountains
have to be a long way off. Here the flat space between the sign
and the mountains enhances the sense of depth. The clouds
also decrease in size as they near the horizon, adding to the
feeling of deep space.

City streets often can be viewed as stages with shallow depressions in the surfaces of buildings. People move in and out of these shallow spaces like actors on a stage.

Shallow space

Like deep space, shallow space is a relative term. It can vary from the crack in a brick to a window in a wall to a theater stage. We can easily contrast the shallow space of a bookshelf with the much deeper space of the block on which we live.

Shallow spaces can often be identified because of the shadows which are cast in them. This contrast of values enables us to see the relief and therefore the space involved, however slight. When the light changes, the sense of space might disappear and the surface tends to become flat.

Artists who sculpted the frieze figures in ancient Greece used shallow space to great advantage but so do contemporary sculptors who work in *low relief.*

Protrusions above any surface into the surrounding shallow space produce a roughness that can be felt and we call it *texture.* Depressions into any surface allow space to enter the surface and also produce texture.

Shadows indicate the depth of the space on the cast surface of this building. Though the design is abstract, the artist had the same concern with shallow space (low relief) as the sculptors who worked on the Parthenon in Athens.

26

1. Molded paper packing material is useful because it takes up space.
2. The closed windows and the fire escape are shallow depressions and protrusions on the surface of a building.
3. Grout lines in brick walks are often shallow depressions.
4. Store shelves are little shallow spaces for cans and boxes.
5. Woven baskets have a textured surface, indicating shallow space.
6. Doors have low relief and therefore occupy shallow space.

Looking into spaces

Space is not only *around* things, it is also *inside* things. Often, when we look into some form or object we cannot see details because the space inside looks dark or even black. The reason is, the light source inside is shut off and the space appears dark by contrast with the outside of the form.

Cast shadows can also help define the shape of inside space. Curved shadows indicate a round form while window and door frames cast a straight-edged shadow. When light is not directly from the sun or other single strong light source, the edge of the shadows might seem soft and gradually change from light to dark.

At night, the inside space of a house appears much lighter than the dark spaces outside because it is illuminated artificially. Become aware of the changes in value and it will become easier to paint or draw the interior space.

Looking down into a circular stairwell (there is a fountain at the bottom) illustrates the darkening values as you look deeper into the open space.

The round opening of this old cannon barrel casts a round shadow on the rounded interior.

The car is entering a downtown garage which is very dark inside. The value change is gradual as you look deeper inside because the light source is indirect and not directly from the sun.

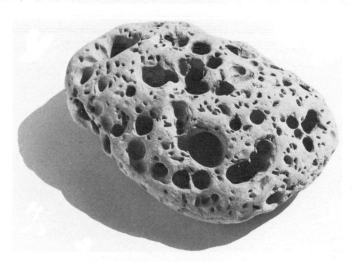

Looking into the holes in this rock, you can see slight detail in some places but all detail is obscured in others where the light source is completely blocked out. The result is void of light — or black.

Stark and jagged against a lighter valued sky, an old cypress tree presents a strong positive statement. Notice the way the negative space eats into and through the overall form of the tree. The negative space also slashes its way into the positive spaces of the dark tree shapes.

A landing jet is easy to pick out from its surrounding negative space.

Since sculpture is designed in three dimensions, it is often viewed as a positive space surrounded by air, which is negative space.

Positive and negative space

When three-dimensional forms are standing alone, it is easy to notice the space around them. The statue is a form occupying positive space and the area around it is considered negative space. A lone tree, sailboat, automobile or house occupies positive space.

If you become acutely aware of negative space, you can see it eat into the positive form. It cuts, stabs, meanders or plunges into a statue, dry tree or bridge.

Sculptors and architects are deeply concerned with this negative space because it is as important to them as the form of the sculpture or building itself.

Setting a strong form against the sky is the easiest way to separate the positive from negative space. If the background is cluttered, the negative space is more difficult to define.

A carved wooden decoration occupies shallow three-dimensional positive space. The negative space can be seen around the carving and between it and the wall. It is often easier to identify negative space when sky is the background.

31

WAYS TO OBSERVE THREE-DIMENSIONAL SPACE

The artists of the Renaissance were intrigued with describing three-dimensional space in their paintings. They looked hard at nature trying to observe ways to show depth. When they discovered such ways, they delighted in stressing perspective in their work.

You can become more sensitive to space and depth perception by learning to see how nature does it for you.

Overlapping shapes and forms

As soon as we use words like "in front of" or "behind," we are talking about space. When one leaf overlaps another, depth is indicated. When one person stands behind another or when a tree is in front of a building, space is instantly felt.

Watch a person walking *in front of* a wall, a dog running *between* trees, one car parked *in front of* another, or cans *on* a supermarket shelf. Overlapping shapes or forms produce a feeling of space or three dimensionality.

One sign overlaps the next all the way down the street. Each palm tree does likewise. Other indications of depth are also present to emphasize the feeling of space.

You can tell which parts of this plant are nearest to your eye — and which are farther away, by simply being aware of the overlapping forms.

The apple is closest, the orange next and the banana is farthest away. This can be determined by noticing the overlapping sequence.

The space occupied by these trumpet players can be noticed
because of the overlapping of horns and people. You can easily
see which is closest to you and which is farthest away.

Lockers of the same size seem to shrink as they line a wall that is running away from the camera.

Sprinters of similar size spring from the blocks. However the dash man in the farthest lane seems smaller because he is farther away. The overlapping of the figures also adds to the feeling of depth and space.

Decrease in size

It seems ridiculously simple to say that the farther away from you an object is, the smaller it appears. But this is one of the basic concepts in depicting space. Objects known to be the same size (like telephone poles) seem to get smaller as they recede into the background.

Downtown skyscrapers look like toy blocks from five miles away but become larger at one mile. When standing beside a fifty-story structure, the building seems enormous.

Notice how small people look when a block away or even on the other side of the field. As they get closer, they also seem to grow in size.

It's a simple observation and an easy way to show depth in a painting or design.

Looking up the side of a building, the windows diminish in size as they loom to the top. If the building were tall enough, the lines would converge to a single dot at the top.

Cattle are about the same size but seem to almost disappear as they get farther away from your eye. The equal-sized fence posts are perpendicular to your vision (equidistant from your eyes) and therefore are seen as being the same height. If they ran away from your vision, they would also decrease in size.

When ceiling, floor and wall lines are extended, they will all meet at a point in the glaring white window. The linear perspective the architects have incorporated is easily recognizable.

Looking up a flagpole emphasizes linear perspective.

The parallel black lanes on a straight section of interstate highway seem to converge in the distance. When long distances are involved, the space seems very deep.

While walking across a bridge you can come face to face with linear perspective. The longer the bridge, the closer the converging lines come together.

Linear perspective: one point

Trying to show three-dimensional space on a two-dimensional surface (a painting or drawing) is perspective. Using lines to show depth is called linear perspective.

During the Renaissance, Italian artists discovered that when parallel straight lines run away from the observer, they seem to converge at a point. We call it a vanishing point because the objects seem to disappear at this point. When they drew lines coming to a single point, they created a feeling of depth.

Close one eye and you can see just like the camera lens. Observe the converging lines all around you as you look along a wall of lockers, up the side of a building or along the street on the way home.

Linear perspective is an old way of seeing space but it is still one of the best ways to show depth in your drawing and painting.

39

The leading edges of these parallel platforms lead to one vanishing point, but the perpendicular lines that divide the sections lead to a second point. The eye level is below the bottom of the photo.

Rectangular boxcars are standing at an angle to the direction of the camera, so two vanishing points are evident. The eye level is above the top edge of the photo.

PARALLEL LINES RUNNING AWAY FROM YOU

PARALLEL LINES PERPENDICULAR TO YOUR LINE OF VISION

EYE LEVEL

A

LINE OF SIGHT

PARALLEL LINES, BUT THEY ARE AT AN ANGLE TO YOUR LINE OF SIGHT

EYE LEVEL

VANISHING POINTS

(B)

Linear perspective: two point

While one-point perspective uses lines that lead to a single point and shows objects that are square with your line of sight (A), two-point perspective can deal with objects sitting at odd angles with your eye (B).

Books, boxes, benches or buildings that are askew from your direct line of sight can be shown in this way. When objects are drawn correctly, the sense of space and actual occupation of space in depth is felt. The eye level (everything in a line that is level with your eye when looking straight ahead of you) is shown by drawing a line parallel to the top edge of your paper. The vanishing points are located on the eye level (B).

Systems for correctly depicting such spatial concepts can become quite complicated. If you look carefully and notice the way edges and lines slope and slant, you are well on your way to observing the cues that create perspective — the feeling of three-dimensional space.

41

Foreground shrubs and rocks are sharply focused and dark in value, contrasting dramatically with the distant mountains which are light valued and flat. Such value contrast pushes the peninsula forward.

Cross-country runners jog into the beach fog ahead. The leading runner is almost enveloped by the fog and loses all identifying detail. A feeling of great depth and space results.

Aerial perspective: the smog can help

To show that space exists between himself and the distant mountains, Leonardo da Vinci painted a light-value haze that seemed to obliterate details and push the mountains farther away.

Objects that are close by generally seem to be in sharper focus, contain more detail and are more intensely colored. Things in the distance are usually unclear, have little detail, seem flat and are lighter in value than similar objects close by.

Observing these features around you is easy. Haze, fog or smog can push objects farther away and can help you become aware of space.

The large city in the distance looks small because of the open space between the photographer and it. Compared to closer objects, it appears pale and contains no detail at all.

Distant objects appear higher. . .

Experiment by looking at your feet. Now slowly start to look at the floor in front of your feet and raise your head, looking at all the things your eye contacts, until you are looking straight ahead. You are now looking at your eye level — all things even in height with your eyes.

Everything below your eye level, as your eye was covering the ground from your feet to the distance, seemed to get higher as they got farther away. Look at the desks in a classroom — the closer ones are lower than the ones farther away. Look at the objects in a still life, forcing yourself to see only the bases of the things where they meet the surface of the table. The base of the closest object is lowest in the setup, while the bases of things get higher as they go back on the table.

All things *below* your eye level will appear to do this, but if the objects are *above* your eye level, they will act in an opposite way, getting lower as they go away from you. Think of street lights, clouds, or a line of helicopters or birds.

The base of the tree nearest you is lowest in the photo while the bases of succeeding trees appear higher as they recede into the forest.

The lowest fountain spout is nearest to you while the highest one is farthest away.

45

Looking **up at** *a flag and trophy gives them both dramatic impact.*

A point of view: looking at, looking up at, or looking down on things

Artists during the Baroque times delighted in distorting perspectives and looking at things from peculiar points of view. A building appears different from the street than from the roof next door because the angle or point of view determines how it will appear in space.

Your car looks different when it is on the grease rack because you are not used to looking up at it. A baseball field looks different when you are standing on the pitcher's mound than when you are looking down on it from the stands. A mountain looks huge when you are at its base, but the valley looks huge when you are on the top of the mountain.

Look around you carefully and try to see what happens to objects or people when you change your point of view. When you looked down on the street from a high window, do you remember how funny it is to see people walking?

Conventional spatial relationships change as your angle or point of view changes. Artists or photographers can take advantage of this to produce dramatic or provocative spatial concepts.

We don't often look directly **down on** *our dishes, but the changing point of view makes you feel suspended over them, like a spider. Notice how the shadows help determine their size and the space they occupy.*

Looking obliquely at the flower pots is only one way to see all
of them. Many photos could be taken directly at them, or
down on them (or from the inside of them). The point of view
determines how they will appear in space.

Trash cans are round, but when looked at from an angle, the opening appears oval in shape. The bottoms are more curved than the tops.

What happens to circles and cylinders

When you look straight down on a round plate it is circular in shape. But when you look at the same plate obliquely or from an angular point of view, it no longer seems perfectly round but becomes a flattened oval shape. How flat it appears depends on your eye level: the closer it is to your eye level, the flatter the oval looks.

Since cylinders have circles at either end, they act the same as the round plate. If the cylinder is below your eye level, its bottom will be rounder than its top, which is closer to your eye level.

Dishes and cup are round but provide oval shapes when viewed from an oblique angle.

Both the bottles and the wine rack provide excellent examples of cylinders viewed from different angles. Top ones are at eye level while the bottom row is **below** eye level.

Round wheels appear oval from this angle.

A setting sun provides back lighting and the ranges of mountains and row of vegetation turn to flat shapes (almost like cardboard cutouts). Overlapping of these shapes produces some feeling of depth, but it is not very strong or accurate.

Interior back lighting reduces three-dimensional human forms to flat, two-dimensional shapes.

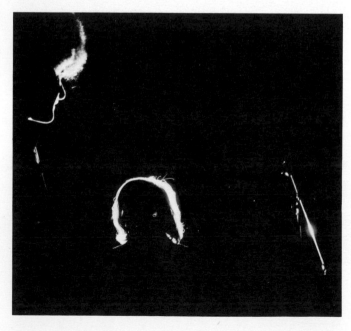

The effect of light on space

In order for space to be seen correctly, light is necessary. As with color, if light is not present or is present in a diffused or filtered way, space may seem flattened or non-existent.

Space is most accurately seen when the light source (sun or light bulb) is above or to the side of observed objects. Depth also is felt quite correctly when the light source is behind you. In all of these cases the objects will throw shadows that will help your eyes read the depth and space.

When the source of light is in front of you and shining *at* you, it is called *back lighting* and it tends to flatten space. You look *at* a sunset (source of light) and objects between you and the sun become flattened silhouettes. The less light, the flatter the objects and space become.

Even diffused light through fog or thick clouds creates a flatter look than full sunlight would produce. Dusk or dawn are difficult times to drive your car because accurate depth perception is hindered by the lack of light.

Other pages in the book will show you objects in full light; but, here you can become aware of the effect that a lack of sufficient light can produce.

Dramatic back lighting turns houses, clouds and trees into silhouettes — flat and lacking depth.

The afternoon sun, back lighting this deep canyon, tends to flatten the rock walls which in reality are deeply cut. To illustrate the flattening of space, the river is over 800 feet down in the canyon and about a quarter of a mile away; yet, it appears to be a short distance beyond the foreground rock and shrub.

Tree branches that are closest to the wall cast the sharpest shadows, while branches far removed from the same wall are extremely fuzzy.

Several aspects of space can be felt in this photo. Space exists **between** the lattice work (not shown) and the wall. The wall occupies space because the shadows **bend** as they go around the corner. The details of the house next door are lost because of the distance.

Low relief (shallow protrusions into space) can be felt when oblique light (flat angled light) rakes across the surface.

Shadows and space

If insufficient light tends to flatten space (see pages 50-51), then an abundance of light should emphasize space. And it does! Because bright light will cause objects in its path to cast shadows, our eye will read the results as space between object and shadow.

Shadows make a ball look *round* to us (so it occupies space). Sunlight and shadow give *form* to a tree, giving it volume. Texture and shallow relief can be *felt* by our eyes because of surface shadows.

An airplane flying overhead on a sunny day casts a shadow on the ground. A moth makes a darting shadow on the wall. Our body creates a recognizable shadow on the sidewalk. There is space between the objects and their shadows and with a bit of careful observation, you can feel the *amount* of space that exists.

Generally, the closer the object is to the wall or ground the sharper the shadow will be. The flying airplane casts a fuzzy shadow while your own shadow has a sharper edge.

*Can you feel the **space** between the hanging planter and its shadow on the wall?*

Light source is at the left of the jar, causing it to cast a shadow to the right. Notice the detailed definition of the lip as indicated by the shadows. Study all of the jar's features as developed by the shadows.

53

Value contrasts and
color can show space

Value contrasts (differences in lights and darks) are generally the result of light striking different surfaces that have space between them. Such contrasts can *push* some objects forward or force others back. Black and white photographs make use of value contrasts to show depth of space, as our eyes interpret those contrasts and indicate the amount of space. Shadows are also seen as changes in value and, as such, indicate depth.

Artists use this concept to emphasize space or to flatten it out. They can also fool your eyes into seeing space where it does not really exist. You can emphasize space by strong contrasts in dark and light; working light against dark or dark against light.

Color is also an indicator of space. Warm colors seem to come forward and cool colors tend to recede. The nerves in our eyes relate these sensations to our brain and we see space. Painters can make use of these facts to give their work a strong feeling of depth. . . or they can play tricks on our eyes and deceive us into reading depth where none really exists.

Dramatic value contrasts not only give the drummer form but cause him to stand forward from the background. Notice the sequence of light against dark and dark against light.

Leaves in this hedge are all the same color of green, but their values differ because of the light reflected. Such value contrasts indicate that space exists between the layers of leaves.

54

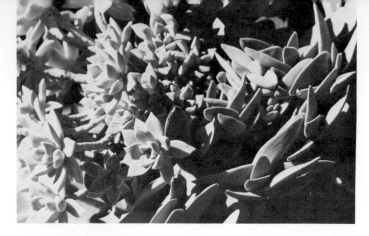

Bright light forces some leaves forward while darker valued leaves allow us to feel the space between them.

Jackson Pollock's painting is flat, yet the contrast in values causes our eyes to see depth of space — like steamers floating in air. The colors might help emphasize this feeling of space (or throw us into confusion if cool colors are on top). Overlapping of linear patterns emphasizes the feeling of depth to our eyes, and so does the title, **Full Fathom Five.** *Jackson Pollock, 1947. Oil on canvas, 50 7/8 x 30 1/8. Collection, the Museum of Modern Art, New York. Gift of Peggy Guggenheim.*

SPACE IN WHICH WE LIVE

Rooms

Walls, ceilings and floors provide limits to space, enclosing the areas in which we spend time. We eat, study, sleep and watch TV in rooms. Some of us might have our own room — our own space. We decorate the walls of our space with favorite things and try to make it as pleasant as possible.

Walls enclose us, give us privacy and make us feel secure. They separate spaces but windows and doors allow us to pass from one space to another or allow the outside space to come in. Some people like their spaces to be less confining and have many windows. Others prefer to be sheltered from the outside space as much as possible. Even our cars have spaces reserved for them. Man's first enclosed spaces were provided by nature but now they are built in an unending variety of shapes, sizes and combinations. We stack them on top of each other or put them in rows on a street. We paint or paper them, spend time to make them comfortable and retreat to them to be alone with our thoughts. Rooms are really living spaces for people.

We leave our living space at home and enter a mobile space, enclosed by steel and glass, and move to school.

Schools are also made up of enclosed spaces, some large and open, others small and more confining. We attend classes in spaces, play basketball in spaces, eat lunch in spaces, walk through long enclosed spaces to get to more rooms. We seem to require spaces that are designed for every needed purpose, whether at home, at school or at work.

Yet, there are some who have shunned all such enclosed spaces, preferring to live in one large outside space.

Cities and streets

Where many people are gathered together in a community, we have developed towns and cities. To collect more people in these spaces, man has devised ways to keep order. We line up our enclosed spaces on either side of streets, giving each building a number. We pile enclosed spaces on top of each other and call them apartments. We can stack them in levels of two. . . or up to a hundred. We can make them cover a city lot . . . or a city block.

Office buildings can hold thousands of people in their ordered spaces. We sometimes work in huge spaces, sometimes in confining spaces. We type, sell, sew, draw, calculate, build, rivet, nail, saw, buy, clean and study in enclosed spaces. Our cities are accumulations of occupied spaces.

To move around in cities, we must have passageways. Streets are both the separator and the unifier of the scattered spaces in which we live and work. People live across the street from you, yet you also drive on streets to visit friends.

A freeway can be a real divider of communities, and still it unifies one part of the city with another. You use the street to get to school, to travel to the library, the store, or your place of worship. You drive a car on the street . . . or ride your bike . . . or skip along the sidewalks. Streets are connecting corridors . . . distributing branches . . . conveyors on which our mobile spaces move . . . the arteries of the city.

Wide open spaces

If we travel out of our cities . . . on our highways . . . we can find spaces which are more open, less confining. Cities are full of confinements and limits which disappear when we get to open country. Our eyes have unrestricted vision . . . we can see for miles. We can actually see the sky come down to meet the earth. Or so it seems.

The oceans, huge lakes, flat deserts, vast fields, great plains, pasture lands, beaches, playas, marshes and tundras all communicate the feeling of space. There are limits, even to such open spaces . . . hills, mountains, clouds, cliffs or rows of trees. But they do not confine or compress our space as much as walls, buildings or ceilings.

And sometimes the space seems endless . . .

Air space

The ultimate in open space is up. Look at the vastness above you . . . when you are outside. Does it have any limitations at all?

Clouds sometimes limit our vision of it, airplanes or birds fly through it, rain falls from it, and rainbows appear in it. Air space can be gentle or menacing . . . absolutely calm or full of fantastic force. The sun and the moon seem suspended in it. It can appear empty . . . a vast void . . . or filled with a million twinkling lights. It can be warm or cool, friendly or hostile.

Man attempts to encroach upon air space by erecting huge structures to pierce it . . . but such attempts are feeble. His grandest efforts can be scarcely noticed from a winging jet . . . and sometimes not at all from a circling satellite.

There is space without end above us . . . And we call it just that . . . space.

Specific-use spaces

From the day man learned to pile rocks to make walls, he has created enclosed spaces . . . spaces that are used for special needs and events. It is important to be aware of enclosed areas since we spend a large part of our lives in them. Materials, styles and dimensions may change, but the concept of enclosed space is timeless. Architects are concerned with it. Builders are hired to construct it. People must function in it. Worship, business, games, industry, relaxation, family, love, recreation, work and learning require the use of enclosed spaces.

Some enclosed spaces are open to the sky — patios, courtyards, plazas, piazzas, squares, arenas. Others are completely enclosed — churches, rooms, hallways, factories, stores, gyms.

Designers and architects want to make spaces that are perfectly suited to the activity intended to take place in them. They contend that the form of the structure must be the result of its function . . . Look around you to see if that is true for the specific-use spaces that you occupy every day.

Architecture: space in which we live

Architects are designers of spaces! They work to create enclosed areas for living, working, playing, worshipping, or enjoying cultural events. The product of their designing is called architecture.

Architects try to design structures that satisfy the needs of the people who use them, but that is not all. They also want to make them as pleasant as possible. Beauty, texture, form, color and line are designed with great care to produce spaces that enhance the activities that take place in them.

Architecture can be formidable or intimate, inviting or severe, functional or decorative, open or enclosed, angular or organic, international or regional, institutional or folk-art, traditional or experimental, huge or diminutive, high-rise or suburban, industrial or domestic.

Any structure of man which encloses areas used by people for any purpose whatsoever is architecture. How well it is designed is the concern of the architect . . . and you.

67

Sculpture: Designing in space

Three-dimensional constructions, carvings, modelings, or designs are called sculptures. Artists who work with plaster, clay, plastic, steel, ivory, wood, wire, glass, cement and other three-dimensional materials are designers in space. Their creations actually occupy space. You can move around them — or through them. You can feel them. Your eye moves not only up and down on them, but also in and out, forward and back.

Sculptors work in an endless variety of materials, each having its own characteristic feel and appearance.

Such space designs may be huge . . . think of the Statue of Liberty or the Buddha of Kamakura. They may also be small . . . think of jewelry, a scarab, or a Japanese table figurine. They may be any size in between. But all are three-dimensional — occupying space.

Maiastra, *Constantin Brancusi. White marble, 22 inches high; carved limestone pedestal in three sections, 70 inches high. Collection, The Museum of Modern Art, New York. Katherine S. Dreier Bequest.*

68

The Cheyenne (Indian on Horseback), *Frederic Remington.*
Bronze cast sculpture, 21 inches high. Collection, Los Angeles
County Museum of Art, Gift of Mrs. Gladys Letts Pollock.

SUBJECTIVE SPACE

Still Life, *Juan Gris. Oil on canvas, 18 by 25 inches. You know the objects must be on a table, but the artist has changed his concept of space to create a more direct design. Conventional perspective is not indicated. Notice his use of line and flat shapes to depict three-dimensional forms. They are flat, but because they overlap, there is feeling of shallow depth. Collection, Los Angeles County Museum of Art, Gift of George Cukor.*

Previous pages have shown you how a camera views the space around us but a camera is limited in its ability to see. It can only show you what is there, accurately and realistically. Our eyes are like that, too, seeing just what is there. But if our eye is linked with imagination, or with our emotions, we can actually surpass the best camera lens in our ability to deal with space. An artist can create his own space and manipulate it at will.

Cubism and abstractionism: designing space

Cubist artists, like Pablo Picasso and Georges Braque, actually redesigned the space around them. Since they felt that painting was not intended to imitate nature, the feeling of space on their canvases did not have to "feel" like actual space in nature. They literally created their own personal space in the painting. They flattened space, fractured forms, experimented with color, added line where none existed and generally reshaped nature. A cubist painting can show you the top, bottom and side of the same jug in the same painting, something no camera can do.

A cubist or abstractionist canvas can show you an oblique view of a still life on a table, but also allow you to see a direct profile of one vase and the top view of another at the same time in the same painting. Artists today can squash space, distort it, deepen it and change it to suit their personal feelings. Such treatment of space is contrary to nature and the camera lens but contains the imagination and creative energy of the artist.

L'Arlequin Assis, *Juan Gris, 1920. Oil on canvas, 39½ by 28 inches. There is some shadow that indicates space, and so do the curled arms of the chair, but the flat arrangement of shapes in the rest of the painting seems to defy actual depth. A tension develops, which gives the painting a dynamic quality. Collection, Los Angeles County Museum of Art, Estate of David E. Bright.*

Looking through a glass wall into a naturally-lighted mall can produce weird spatial effects. What is reflection (the building behind the camera) and what is viewed directly (banners, beams, signs and people) become inseparably mixed in a congestion of space. Notice that some words are legible and others reversed.

A student artist has created an ambiguous shape that could be flat . . . or could bend back in space . . . or both?

Ambiguous space

Artists have long been intrigued with showing space that is not what it seems to be. If you look carefully around you into reflections, mirrors, distorted glass and metal, you can also notice some ambiguous spaces. Contemporary artists can deceive the eye with line, shape and color and can cause your mind to question whether the space depicted is flat or dimensional. Such optical illusions can be fun but can also form the basis for serious art.

Glass walls of this skyscraper reflect (and distort) the image of a church across the street, behind the camera.

Mylar banners reflect and distort space in a riot of color and shape.

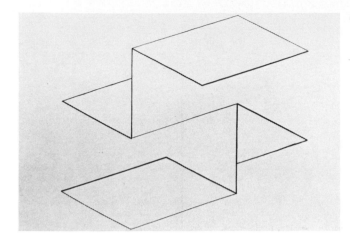

Simple line drawing by a student (following a Josef Albers example) defies a single spatial concept. It can be viewed several ways and is ambiguous in its feeling of space.

Multiple exposures on a single piece of film can cause fascinating spatial results.

Although some of the elements in this painting are convincing in their feeling of depth, a closer inspection might lead us to believe that the artist has invented his own space and can manipulate it at his will. Surrealist painter Rene Magritte produced this painting, **The Liberator** *in 1947. Collection of the Los Angeles County Museum of Art, gift of William Copley.*

Transcending time and space

Artists, both past and present, have at times by-passed the normal presentation of space and time. The High Renaissance painter Raphael in his "Transfiguration" painted two events happening at the same time but in two separate spaces on earth. Early Renaissance artist Masaccio in his "Tribute Money" did him one better, showing three events in one painting, taking place in sequence and in different spaces. Jan Van Eyck painted his "Annunciation" (the angel Gabriel announcing the birth of Christ to Mary) as taking place in a Gothic cathedral. The event took place in Israel about 1 B.C. while the artist shows it taking place in Flanders about 1400 A.D. Other artists throughout history have made similar adjustments in space and time, seeming to transcend the traditional concepts of each.

Surrealist artists attempt to create a deep space in which their illusionary subject matter exists. At first glance, their space appears true enough, but after looking at it carefully, it often becomes extremely subjective and personal — an artistic creation having little relationship to reality. Surrealist artists conceive a twilight zone of space to accommodate their depictions of fantasy.

Although this triptych (painting done on three panels) looks as though the artist painted it from real models in actual locations, it is all quite subjective and transcends actual time and space. The work is titled: **Madonna and Child with Angels, Saints and Patron,** *and was painted by an unknown artist, simply referred to as the Master of the St. Lucy Legend. The artist portrayed the people as living at his own time, around 1475 AD, and in his home country of Flanders, which is now Belgium. The buildings and architectural detail attest to this feeling. However the figure on the left is St. Peter Martyr, who lived during the fourth century AD. Kneeling is the patron, who commissioned the painting during the fifteenth century. The scene in the main panel shows Mary and the Christ-child, who lived in Israel during the first century. The right panel depicts St. Jerome and his lion, both having lived in the fifth century, and not in the country of Flanders. Collection of the Los Angeles County Museum of Art, gift of Anna Bing Arnold.*

INDEX

A camera can help you see space and depth, the same way that your eye can do it. The focus in the first picture is on the fence, while the distant house is out of focus. The second photo was focused on the house, which causes the fence to blur. In camera work, we refer to such space as depth of field. Next time you are in your car, focus your eyes on a speck on the windshield and notice the blur in objects across the street. Now shift your focus across the street and notice what happens to the windshield. Your eye has "felt" the space between the windshield and the objects on the other side of the street.

Although I have traveled in much of the world, have produced several thousand paintings and drawings, have made hundreds of three-dimensional sculptures and ceramic pieces, and have taken thousands of photographs, I never *really* became conscious of SPACE until I worked on this book. I believe the other authors in this series came to the same conclusions regarding their special topics.

And now we want you to become equally aware of space, line, color, value, shape, form and texture. Of course you cannot possibly do this overnight, nor to the degree that each of us were involved in the single element of art. But we want you to become more aware of what is around you — your environment — and how it *really* looks. Once you learn to observe the way we did, you can much more easily transfer your impressions to paper or canvas.

The idea for this series was germinated somewhere in the depths of a Davis Publications staff meeting, and it was my pleasure to help bring it to fruition. I received stimulation and encouragement from the other authors, Joseph Gatto, George

Horn, Al Porter and Jack Selleck, as well as assistance and understanding from my wife, Georgia. All were a great help.

All photographs in the book were taken by the author, except those indicated here: Gary Cloud — 34 (still life), 50 (silhouette), 63 (moon). Los Angeles Chamber of Commerce — 47 (aerial view). Michael Nagata — 6 (wooden construction), 42 (runners), 56 (room), 60 (beach) and 64 (gym). National Aeronautics and Space Administration — 20 (earth). Randy Nelson — 51 (sunset).

Most paintings reproduced are from the collection of the Los Angeles County Museum of Art and are credited as such. Pat North, Registrar, and Phillippa Calnan, Public Information Director, and their staffs were of great help in obtaining prints. John McLeaish of the National Aeronautics and Space Administration in Houston provided the photos of the earth. My thanks also to the crew at Van's Photo Lab for excellent developing and printing and for patiently complying with many requests for hurried work.